FABLES AND TALES PAPERCRAFTS

Written and illustrated by
Jerome C. Brown

Fearon Teacher Aids
a division of
David S. Lake Publishers
Belmont, California

ISBN 0-8224-3155-6
Printed in the United States of America

1.9 8 7 6 5 4 3 2 1

CONTENTS

INTRODUCTION

This book contains directions and patterns for making puppets, masks, sculptures, and other 3-dimensional art projects to enhance the enjoyment of fables and tales. The first four stories presented in this book are from the collection of *Aesop's Fables*. The standard bibliographic title for the last fable is "The Shepherd's Boy and the Wolf," but it is more commonly known as "The Boy Who Cried Wolf." The remaining stories are favorite tales. The copy of the tale you read to your students should make the story come alive. Paul Galdone has retold many of these classic children's tales with colorful and humorous illustrations.

Organizational Helps

Construction paper is used in each papercraft. It is referred to as art paper in the list of materials that accompanies each project. Colors of art paper are suggested but can be changed to suit your needs. Since you will need a pencil, ruler, scissors, glue, and markers or crayons for each project, these items are not listed in each materials list.

For each art project children enjoy, the teacher must spend time in preparation and gathering supplies. This book was designed to minimize that time. Masks and puppets are the most common papercrafts in this book. Special instruction sheets for these projects have been included at the beginning. Once students have mastered the basic format, projects will take less time and explanation. Whole sheets [12" x 18" (30.5 cm x 45.7 cm)], half sheets [9" x 12" (22.9 cm x 30.5 cm)], and quarter sheets [6" x 9" (15.2 cm x 22.9 cm)] of art paper are used whenever possible. This will cut down on the time spent measuring and cutting.

Before beginning each project, reproduce a pattern sheet for each student. Have them cut out all pieces so they can be used for tracing on the colored art paper.

Uses for Papercrafts

Plays and skits can be designed around the masks or puppets. Assign different characters to students and group them to create dialogue and practice a reenactment of the tale.

A coloring page is the first activity listed for each tale. Have the children staple together in a book each of the coloring pages, followed by a sheet of lined writing paper. Have them write a summary of the story, a different ending, or their favorite part. Give the book an appropriate title such as "My Favorite Tales," or "New Endings to Old Favorites."

Display the projects on a mural or bulletin board. Let the students create a background with chalk or paint using an idea from an illustration in a book.

Older children can read and compare various versions of the old familiar tales. They will enjoy making the projects and presenting a skit to a younger group of children.

It is the author's hope that these papercrafts will allow you to bring literature to life in your classroom.

Body and Head for Puppets

Body:

All puppet bodies are made with a 12" x 18" (30.5 cm x 45.7 cm) piece of art paper.

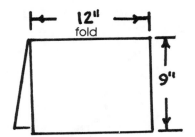

Fold 12" x 18" (30.5 cm x 45.7 cm) into 12" x 9" (30.5 cm x 22.9 cm).

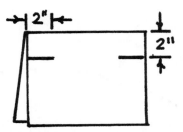

Cut in 2" (5.0 cm) on each side (2" (5.0 cm) from top).

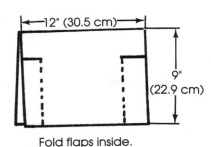

Fold flaps inside.

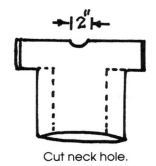

Cut neck hole.

Head and Neck:

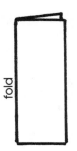

Figure A

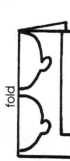

Figure B

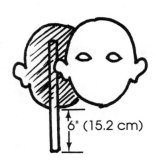

6" (15.2 cm)

Figure C

Figure D

Fold paper for head and neck lengthwise (fig. A). Use the color listed on the project page. Trace and cut two heads and two 1" x 10" (2.5 cm x 25.4 cm) neck strips (fig. B). Cover 1" x 10" (2.5 cm x 25.4 cm) cardboard strip with the two art paper strips to make the neck. Glue the neck between the two heads allowing 6" (15.2 cm) to extend (fig. C). Insert neck into hole on top of body and glue front and back of body together (fig. D). Finish puppet following directions on project page.

Fables & Tales Papercrafts © 1989 David S. Lake Publishers

Head Pattern for Puppets

Reproduce and give each child one pattern or make several sturdier patterns out of tagboard to keep and reuse each time your class makes puppets.

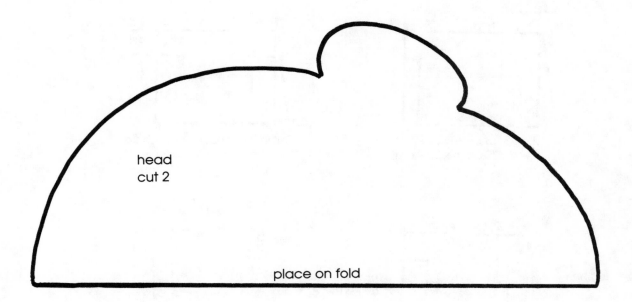

head
cut 2

place on fold

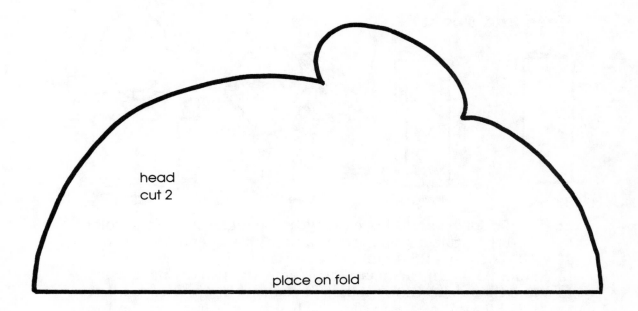

head
cut 2

place on fold

Fables & Tales Papercrafts © 1989 David S. Lake Publishers

DIRECTIONS FOR MAKING
Masks

Fold paper for head and neck lengthwise (fig. A). Use color listed on project page. Trace and cut out two heads and two 1" x 10" (2.5 cm x 25.4 cm) strips (fig. B). Be sure to trace eye holes also. Leave head folded and cut out eye holes. Cut through dotted line to make cutting the small hole easier (fig. C). To make neck, cover 1" x 10" (2.5 cm x 25.4 cm) cardboard strip with art paper strips. Glue neck between the two heads allowing 6" (15.2 cm) to extend (fig. D).

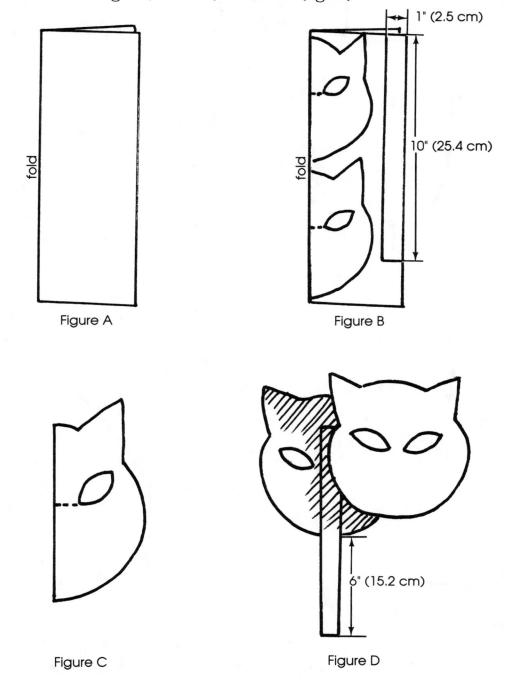

Figure A   Figure B

Figure C   Figure D

The Lion and the Mouse

Fables & Tales Papercrafts © 1989 David S. Lake Publishers

The Lion and the Mouse
(Lion Sculpture)

Materials

- Stapler

Art Paper:

- Brown 9" x 12" (22.9 cm x 30.5 cm) mane, tail, hair
- Yellow
  9" x 12" (22.9 cm x 30.5 cm) cylinder
  12" x 18" (30.5 cm x 45.7 cm) head, legs, tail
- Black scraps for nose

Figure B

Procedure

1. Trace and cut out all pattern pieces noticing which ones are to be placed on the fold.

2. On flat 9" x 12" (22.9 cm x 30.5 cm) yellow paper, glue on mane, front legs, face of lion, forehead hair, and nose (fig. B).

3. Add details with black marker or crayon.

4. Shape into a cylinder and staple in the back at the top and bottom.

5. Glue hind legs and tail on the back side of cylinder so they extend out the sides (fig. A).

Figure A

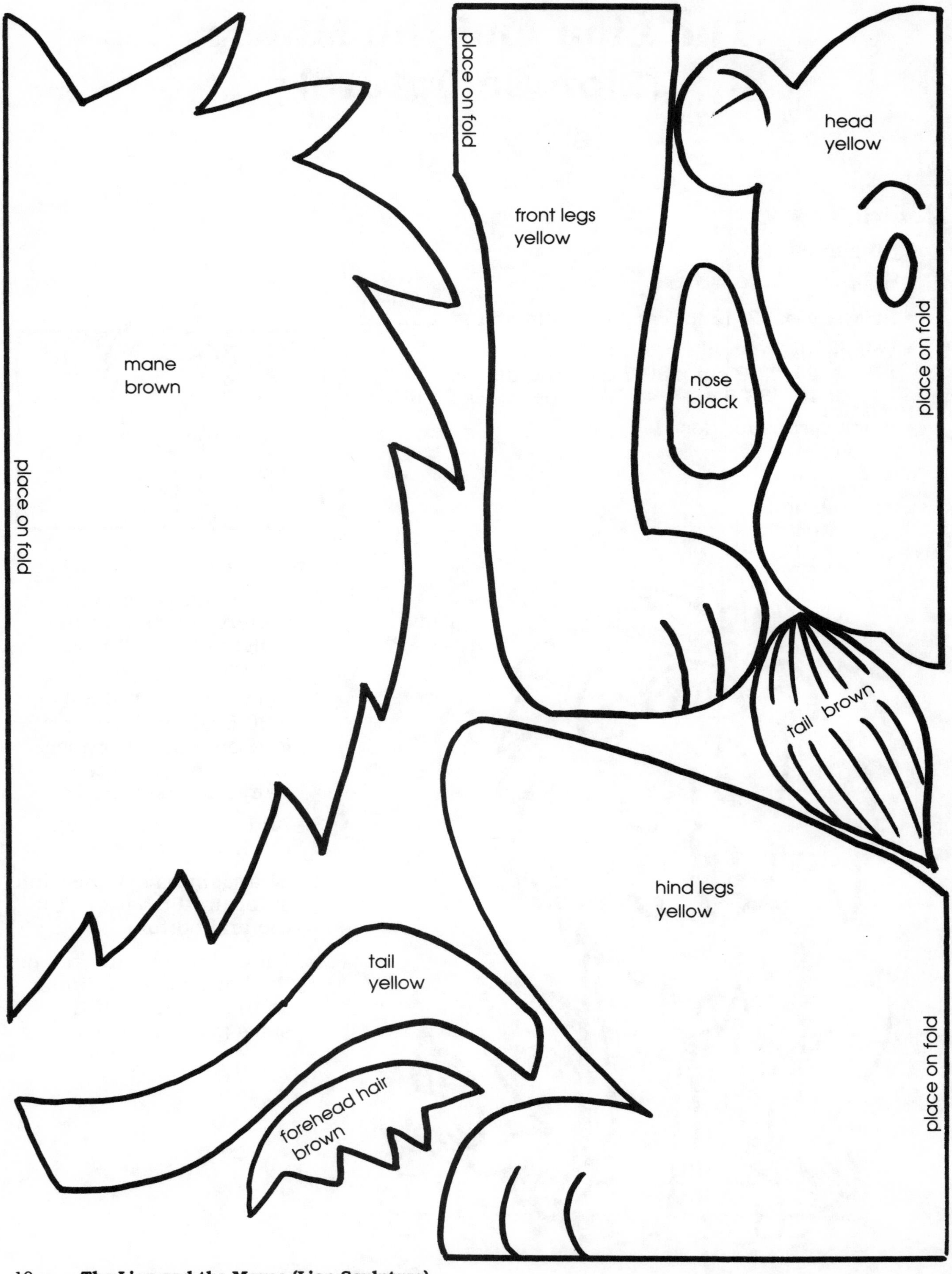

place on fold

front legs
yellow

head
yellow

nose
black

mane
brown

place on fold

tail brown

place on fold

hind legs
yellow

tail
yellow

forehead hair
brown

place on fold

10   **The Lion and the Mouse (Lion Sculpture)**

Fables & Tales Papercrafts © 1989 David S. Lake Publishers

The Lion and the Mouse
(Mice Patterns)

WALNUT MOUSE

Materials

- Half of a walnut shell
- Gray or silver spray paint
- Gray pipe cleaner for tail
- Gray 4" x 4" (10.2 cm x 10.2 cm) art paper
- Two small plastic eyes

Procedure

1. Spray shell with paint and let it dry.
2. Glue pipe cleaner to the inside of the walnut shell.
3. Cover the bottom opening of the shell with art paper. Place a weight on top until dry.
4. Cut gray paper ears and glue on top along with plastic eyes. Add details with black marker or crayon.

FOLDED PAPER MOUSE

Materials

- Gray 6" x 9" (15.2 cm x 22.9 cm) art paper
- Gray pipe cleaner for tail
- Two small plastic eyes

Procedure

1. Trace and cut out mouse pattern on folded art paper.
2. Place the pipe cleaner between the two mouse patterns and glue the mouse together.
3. Glue on plastic eye on each side of the mouse and add other details with markers or crayons.

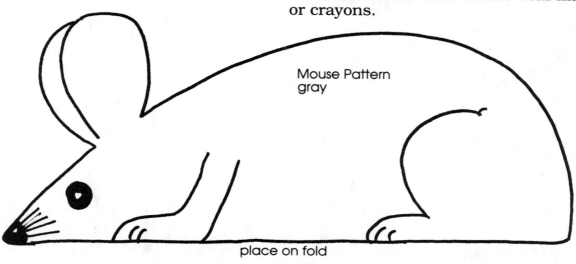

Mouse Pattern
gray

place on fold

The Fox and the Grapes

The Fox and the Grapes (Fox Sculpture)

Materials

- Stapler

Art Paper:

- Brown
    9" x 12" (22.9 cm x 30.5 cm)
    cylinder

    12" x 18" (30.5 cm x 45.7 cm)
    head, legs, paws, tail

- Pink scraps for tongue

- Black scraps for nose

Figure A

Figure B

Procedure

1. Trace and cut out all pattern pieces
   noticing which ones should be placed
   on the fold.

2. On flat 9" x 12" (22.9 cm x 30.5 cm)
   brown paper, glue on front legs, face,
   nose, and tongue (fig. A).

3. Add details with black marker or
   crayon.

4. Shape the paper into a cylinder and
   staple in the back at the top and
   bottom.

5. Glue hind legs and tail on the back of
   the cylinder so they extend out the
   sides (fig. B).

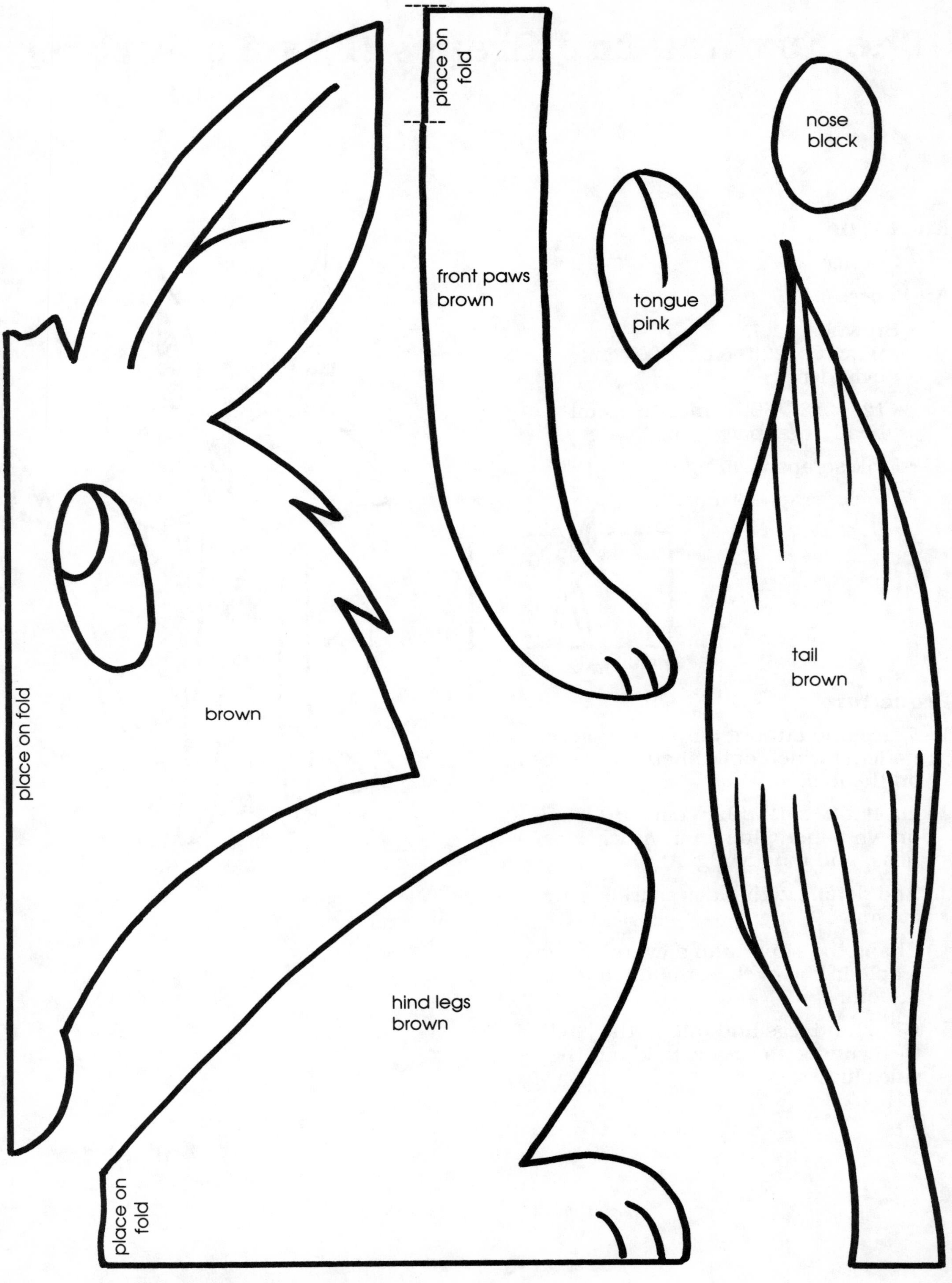

place on fold

place on fold

place on fold

front paws
brown

tongue
pink

nose
black

brown

tail
brown

hind legs
brown

The Fox and the Grapes (Fox Sculpture)

The Fox and the Grapes
(Grapes picture)

The purpose of this project is to learn how
to shade an object to give it a 3-dimensional look.

Figure A

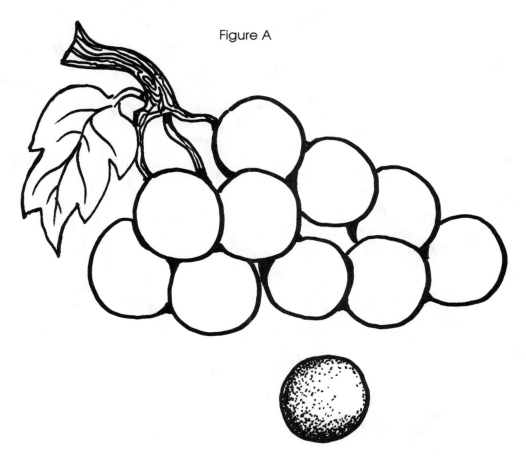

Materials

- Purple or green crayon or chalk
- Copy of grapes picture on page 16 reproduced on 9" x 12" (22.9 cm x 30.5 cm) white art paper
- Black marker

Procedure

1. Outline grapes with black marker.

2. Instruct the students to color darkest, with chalk or crayon, around the edge of each grape, and gradually lighten the color as they reach the center. Leave a white spot for a highlight on the grape. If using crayon, the shading effect will be achieved by applying different amounts of pressure. If using chalk, the shading can be done by blending the chalk with your finger (fig. A).

The Fox and the Grapes (Grapes Picture)

The Tortoise and the Hare

The Tortoise and the Hare Puppets

Figure A

Figure B

Figure C

back detail

Materials

- One 1" x 10" (2.5 cm x 25.4 cm) card-board strip for each puppet

Art Paper:

Hare
- Brown
  12" x 18" (30.5 cm x 45.7 cm) body

  12" x 18" (30.5 cm x 45.7 cm) head, neck, hands, feet, ears
- Blue 9" x 12" (22.9 cm x 30.5 cm) running suit
- Pink 3" x 6" (7.6 cm x 15.2 cm) ears, small circle for nose

Tortoise
- Green
  12" x 18" (30.5 cm x 45.7 cm) body

  12" x 18" (30.5 cm x 45.7 cm) head, neck, feet, tail, hands
- Brown 12" x 18" (30.5 cm x 45.7 cm) shell

Procedure

1. Follow directions on page 5 for tracing, cutting, and gluing body, head, and cardboard neck strip.

2. Trace and cut out remaining pattern pieces.

3. Glue all pieces in place (figs. A and B).

4. Add details with black marker or crayon. Notice the design on the front and back of the turtle's shell (figs. B and C).

Fables & Tales Papercrafts © 1989 David S. Lake Publishers

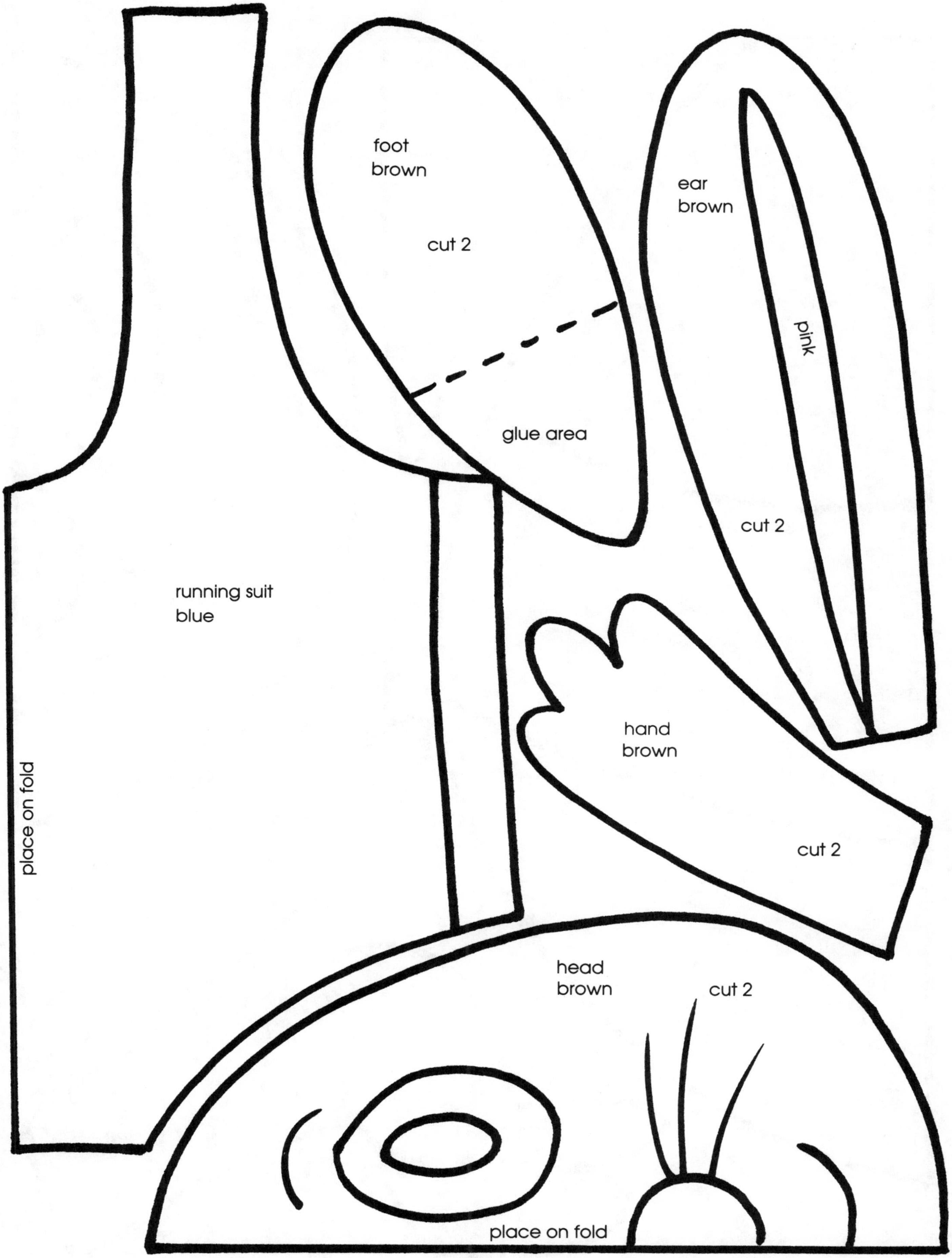

foot
brown

cut 2

ear
brown

pink

cut 2

glue area

running suit
blue

hand
brown

cut 2

place on fold

head
brown

cut 2

place on fold

Fables & Tales Papercrafts © 1989 David S. Lake Publishers

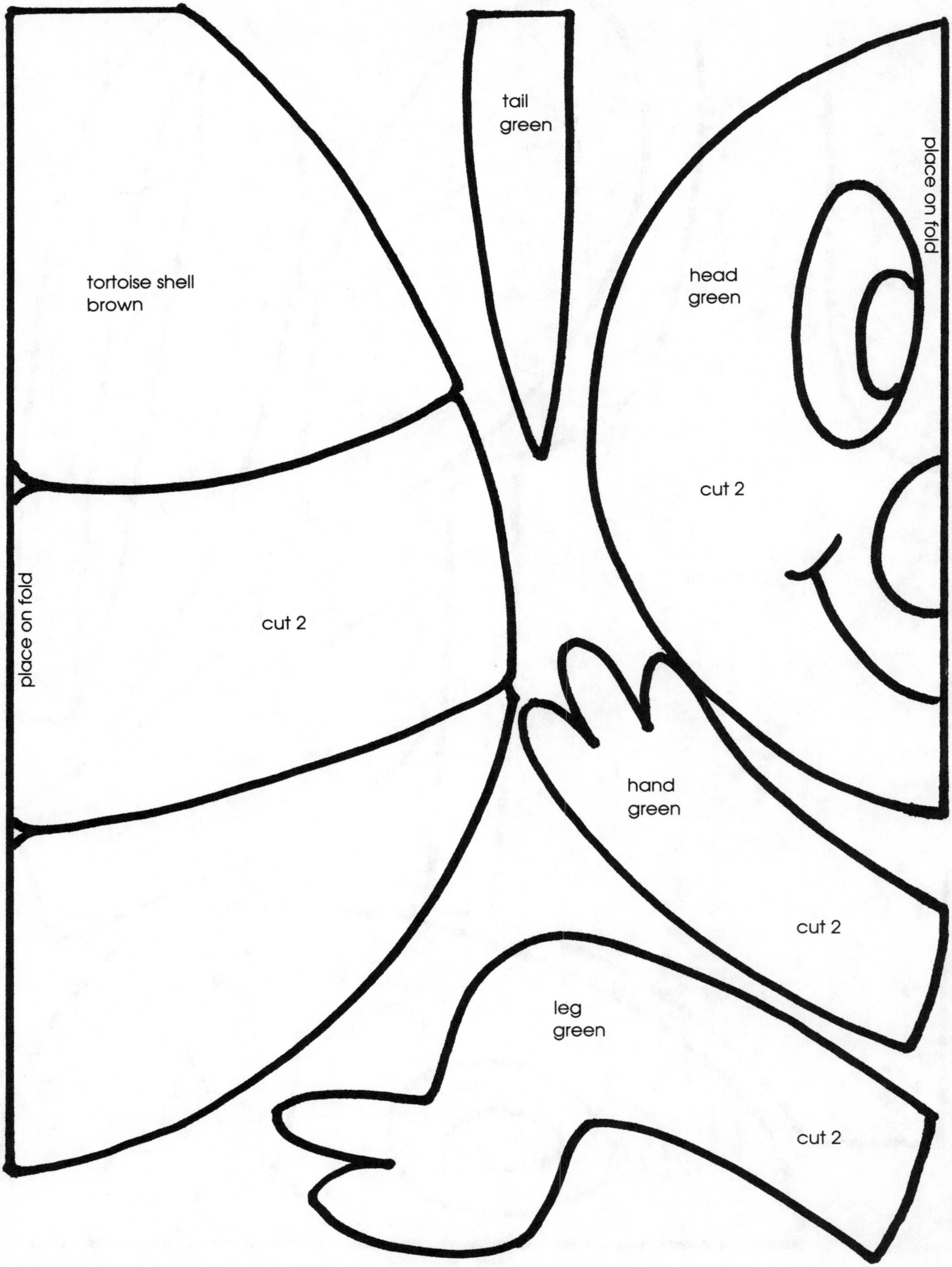

tail
green

tortoise shell
brown

Fables & Tales Papercrafts © 1989 David S. Lake Publishers

place on fold

head
green

cut 2

place on fold

cut 2

hand
green

cut 2

leg
green

cut 2

The Tortoise and the Hare (Tortoise Puppet)

The Shepherd's Boy and the Wolf

The Shepherd's Boy and the Wolf (Boy Mask)

Figure A

Materials

- One 1" x 10" (2.5 cm x 25.4 cm) cardboard strip

Art Paper:

- Pink or brown 12" x 18" (30.5 cm x 45.7 cm) head, neck, nose
- Black 5" x 9" (12.7 cm x 22.9 cm) hair
- Red 2" x 9" (5.0 cm x 22.9 cm) headband

Procedure

1. Follow directions on page 7 for tracing, cutting, and gluing head and cardboard neck strip.
2. Trace and cut out remaining pattern pieces.
3. Glue the pieces in place (fig. A).
4. Draw face details with black marker or crayon.

Fables & Tales Papercrafts © 1989 David S. Lake Publishers

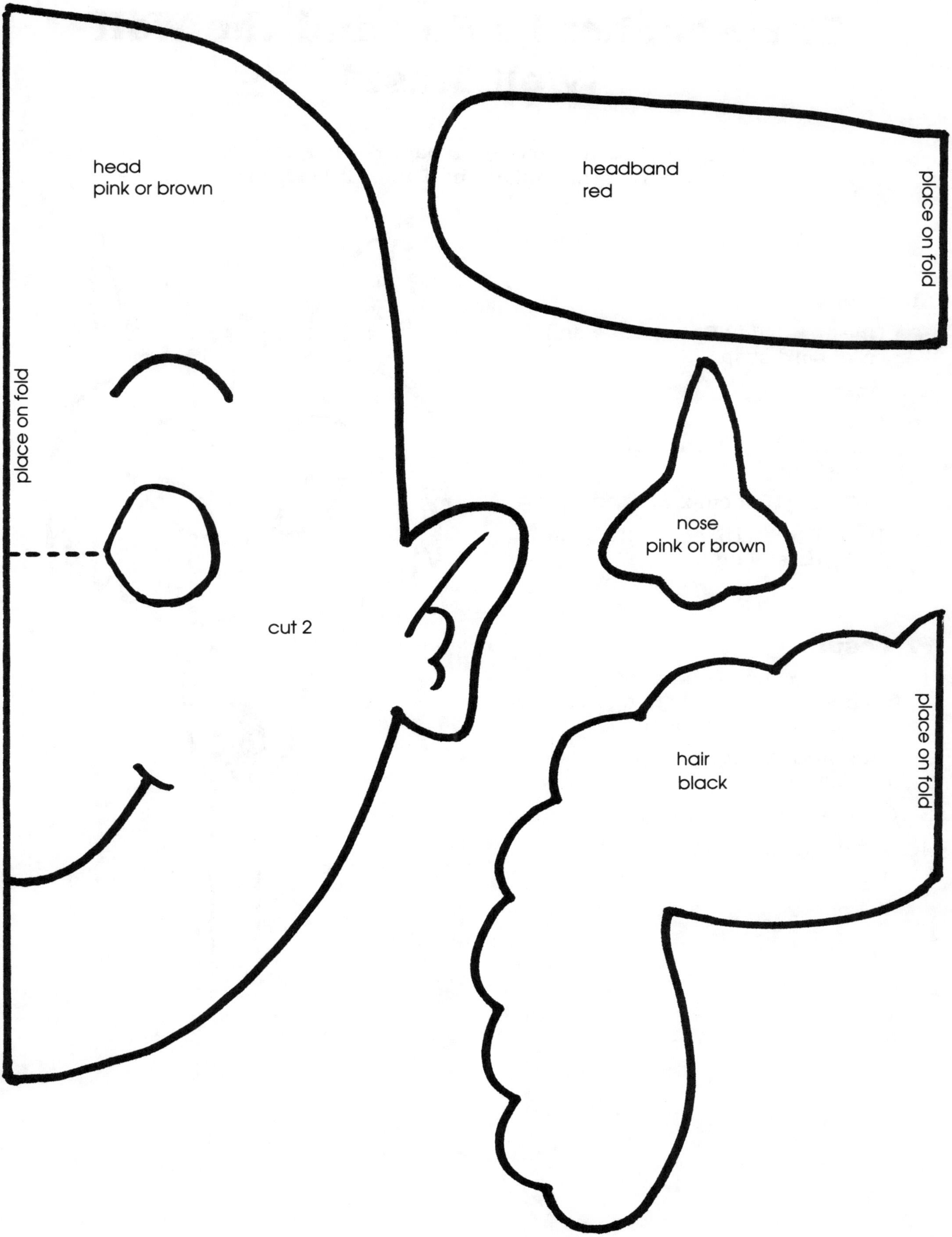

head
pink or brown

headband
red

place on fold

place on fold

cut 2

nose
pink or brown

hair
black

place on fold

The Shepherd's Boy and the Wolf (Wolf Mask)

(Use the pattern pieces on page 64 that are also used for the wolf in The Three Little Pigs.)

Materials

- One 1" x 10" (2.5 cm x 25.4 cm) cardboard strip

Art Paper:

- Brown
  12" x 18" (30.5 cm x 45.7 cm) head, neck

  6" x 9" (15.2 cm x 22.9 cm) ears

- Pink 6" x 9" (15.2 cm x 22.9 cm) inner ears, tongue

Procedure

1. Follow directions on page 7 for tracing, cutting, and gluing head and cardboard neck strip.

2. Trace and cut out remaining pattern pieces.

3. Glue pieces in place (fig. A).

4. Add details with black marker or crayon.

Figure A

Fables & Tales Papercrafts © 1989 David S. Lake Publishers

The Shepherd's Boy and the Wolf
(Sheep Mask)

Materials

- One 1" x 10" (2.5 cm x 25.4 cm) cardboard strip

Art Paper:

- White
    12" x 18" (30.5 cm x 45.7 cm) head, neck

    4" x 7" (10.2 cm x 17.8 cm) ears

Procedure

1. Follow directions on page 7 for tracing, cutting, and gluing head and cardboard neck strip.

2. Trace and cut out ear pattern.

3. Glue ears in place (fig. A).

4. Add details with black marker or crayon.

Figure A

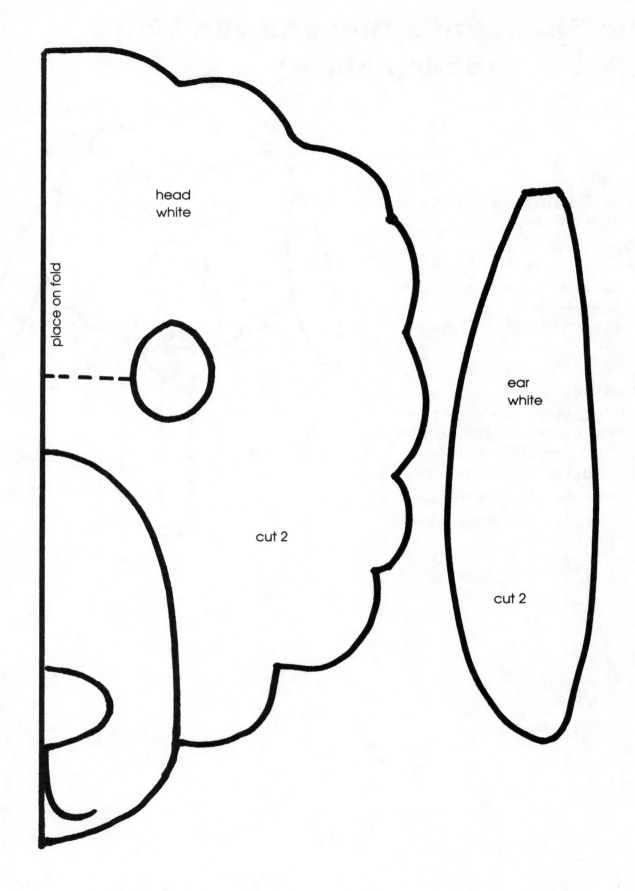

place on fold

head
white

cut 2

ear
white

cut 2

The Frog Prince

The Frog Prince (Queen's Crown)

Materials

- Stapler
- Decorations such as silver foil, star stickers, glitter, yarn

Art Paper:

- Four 1 1/2" x 18" (3.7 cm x 45.7 cm) purple strips
- Two 1 1/2" x 18" (3.7 cm x 45.7 cm) pink strips

Procedure

1. Staple two purple strips together as a band to fit child's head (fig. A).

2. Loop remaining four strips from one side of the headband to the other (fig. B). Staple or glue in place.

3. Add decorations.

purple

pink

purple

Figure A

Figure B

28

Fables & Tales Papercrafts © 1989 David S. Lake Publishers

The Frog Prince (Frog)

Materials

- Stapler

Art Paper:

- Green
  9" x 12" (22.9 cm x 30.5 cm)
  one body

  12" x 18" (30.5 cm x 45.7 cm)
  one body, legs, eye mount

- White and black scraps for eyes

Procedure

1. Trace and cut out all pattern pieces.
2. Unfold both body pieces and cut 1 1/2" (3.7 cm) in on the fold line at both ends (fig. A).
3. Overlap slits and staple (fig. B).
4. Glue all four legs on the inside of the bottom section of the frog (fig. C).
5. Glue eyes together and mount them on the top of the frog (fig. D).
6. Put both frog sections together and staple once on each side (fig. E).

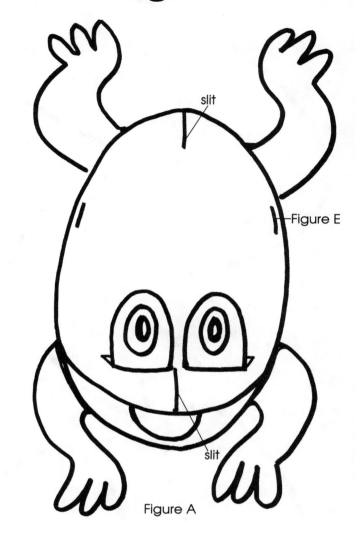

slit

Figure E

slit

Figure A

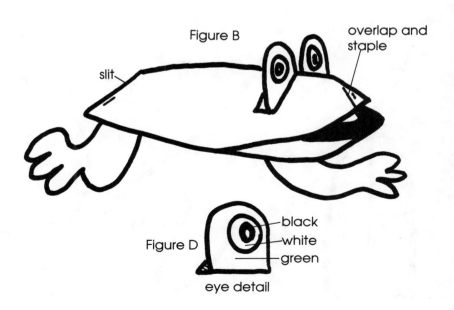

Figure B

overlap and staple

slit

Figure D

black
white
green

eye detail

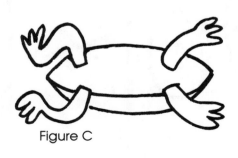

Figure C

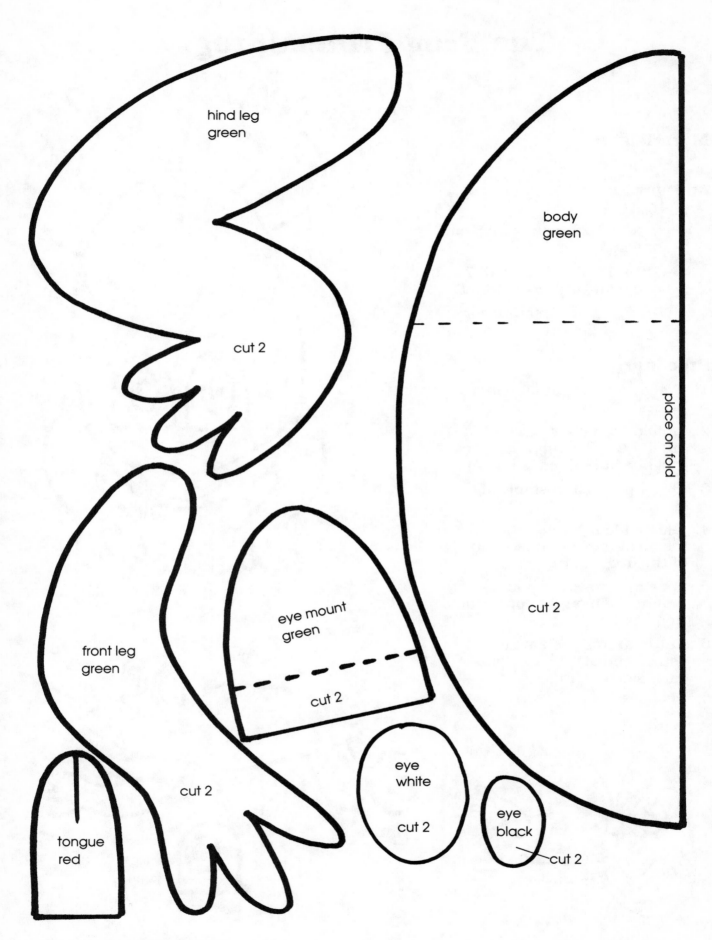

hind leg
green

body
green

cut 2

place on fold

cut 2

front leg
green

eye mount
green

cut 2

eye
white

cut 2

cut 2

eye
black

cut 2

tongue
red

The Gingerbread Boy

The Gingerbread Boy Puppet

Materials

- One 1" x 10" (2.5 cm x 25.4 cm) cardboard strip

Art Paper:

- Brown
    12" x 18" (30.5 cm x 45.7 cm) body

    9" x 12" (22.9 cm x 30.5 cm) head, neck, boots

- Orange 3" x 6" (7.6 cm x 15.2 cm) hat

- Red, purple, blue scraps for trim

Figure A

Procedure

1. Follow directions on page 5 for tracing, cutting, and gluing body, head and cardboard neck strip.

2. Cut end of arms to look like mittens (fig. A).

3. Cut an upside-down V shape at the bottom of the body to form the legs (fig. B).

4. Glue on hat and shoes.

5. Add details on face and body using markers, crayons, or scraps.

Figure B

32

Fables & Tales Papercrafts © 1989 David S. Lake Publishers

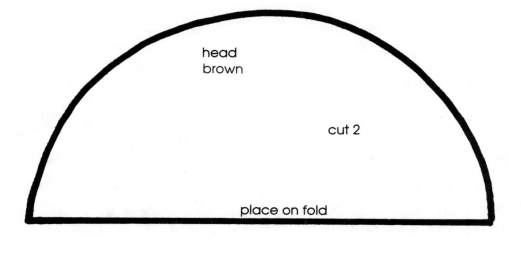

head
brown

cut 2

place on fold

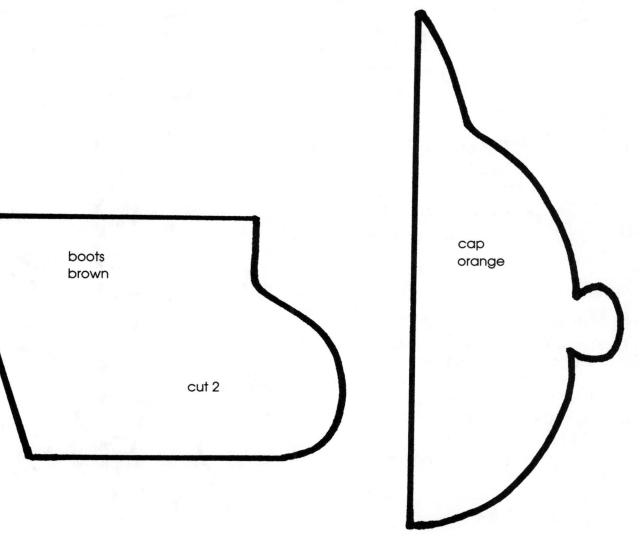

boots
brown

cut 2

cap
orange

The Gingerbread Boy
(Farmer and Fox Puppets)

Figure A

Figure B

Materials

- One 1" x 10" (2.5 cm x 25.4 cm) cardboard strip for each puppet

Art Paper:

Farmer

- Yellow 12" x 18" (30.5 cm x 45.7 cm) body

- Pink or brown 9" x 12" (22.9 cm x 30.5 cm) head, neck, hands

- Brown 6" x 9" (15.2 cm x 22.9 cm) hair, mustache

- Black 9" x 12" (22.9 cm x 30.5 cm) hat, shoes

- Red 4" x 4" (10.2 cm x 10.2 cm) scarf

- Blue 9" x 12" (22.9 cm x 30.5 cm) pants, suspenders

Fox

- Brown
    12" x 18" (30.5 cm x 45.7 cm) body

    12" x 18" (30.5 cm x 45.7 cm) head, neck, feet, paws

- Orange 4" x 7" (10.2 cm x 17.8 cm) tie

- Black scraps for nose and pads on feet

Procedure

1. Follow directions on page 5 for tracing, cutting, and gluing body, head, and cardboard neck strip.

2. Trace and cut out remaining pattern pieces.

3. Glue pieces on head and body (figs. A and B).

4. Add details with black marker or crayon.

34

Fables & Tales Papercrafts © 1989 David S. Lake Publishers

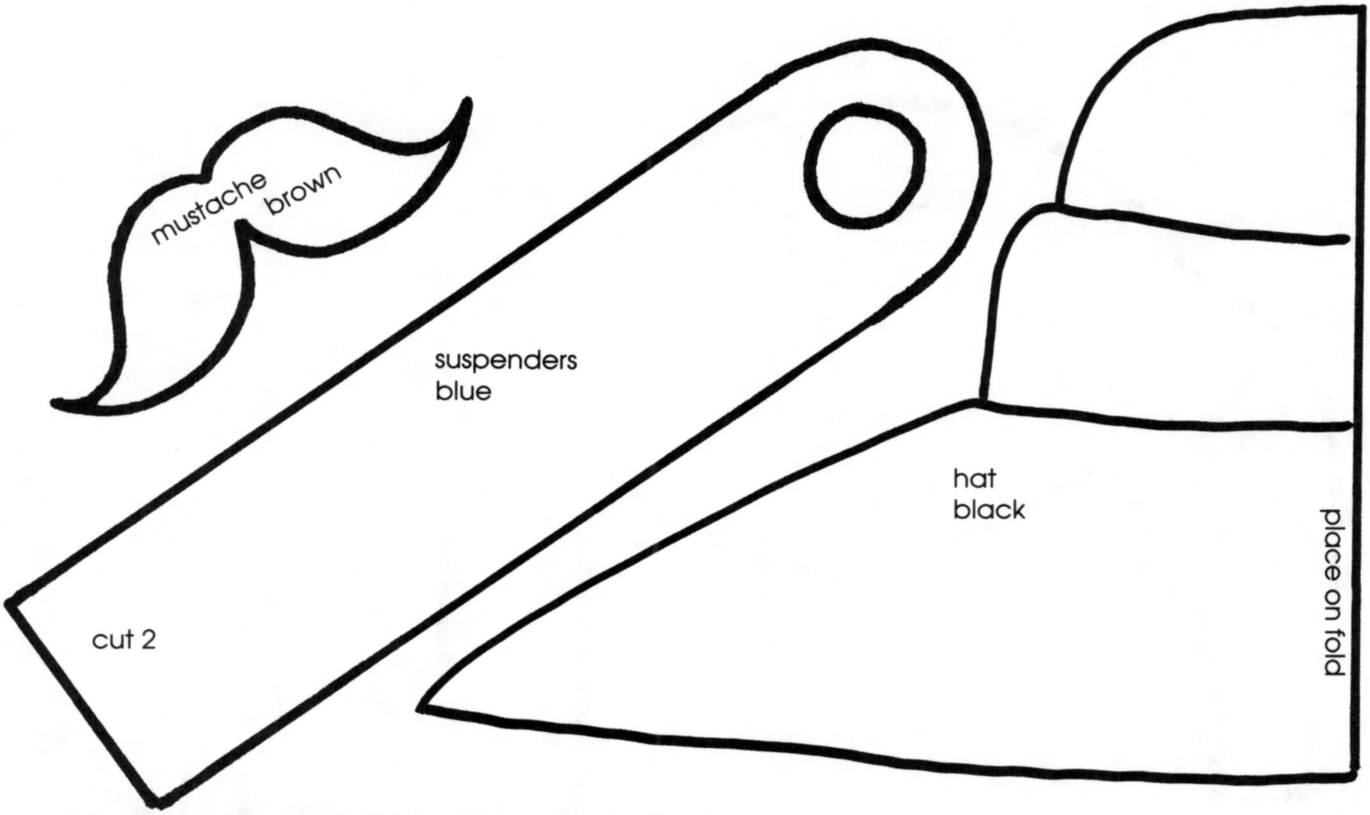

mustache
brown

suspenders
blue

cut 2

hat
black

place on fold

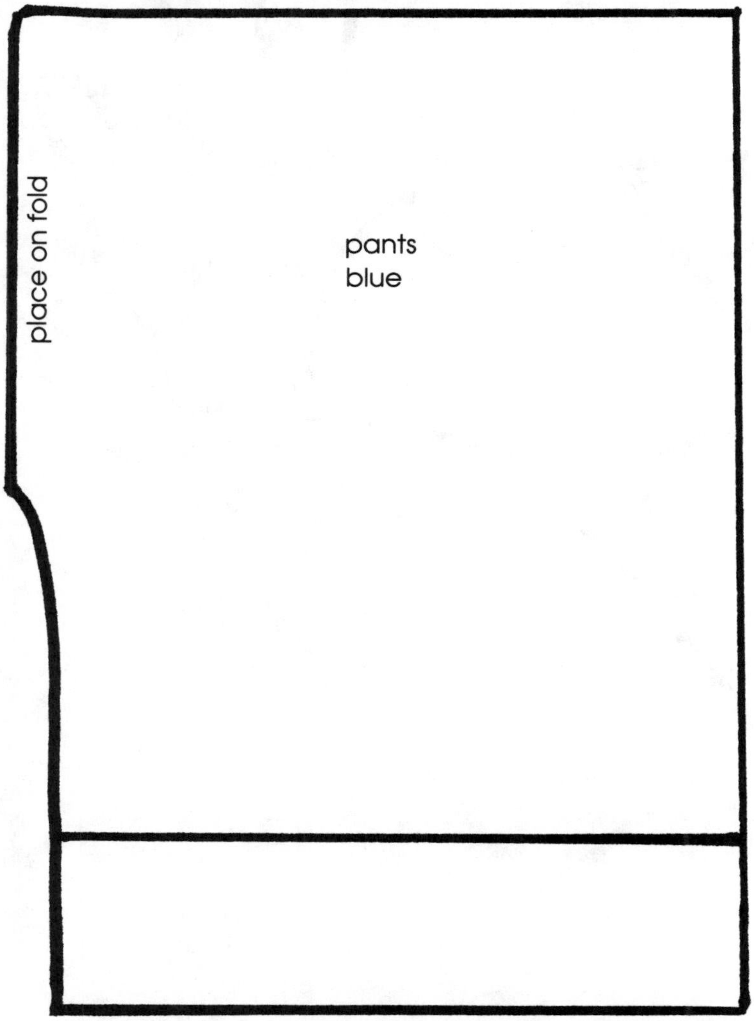

Use head pattern on page 6.

place on fold

pants
blue

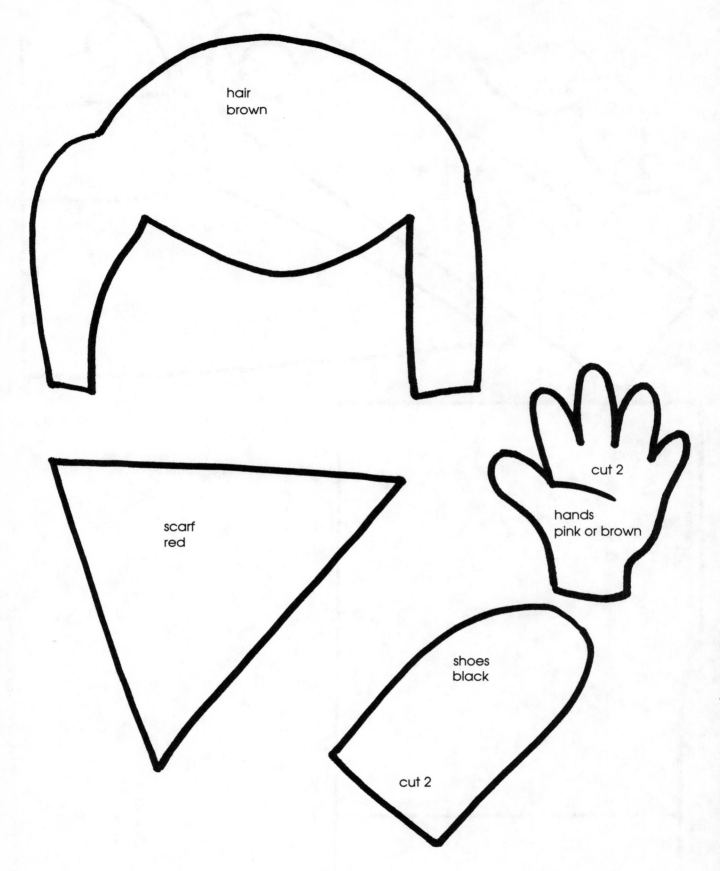

hair
brown

scarf
red

cut 2

hands
pink or brown

shoes
black

cut 2

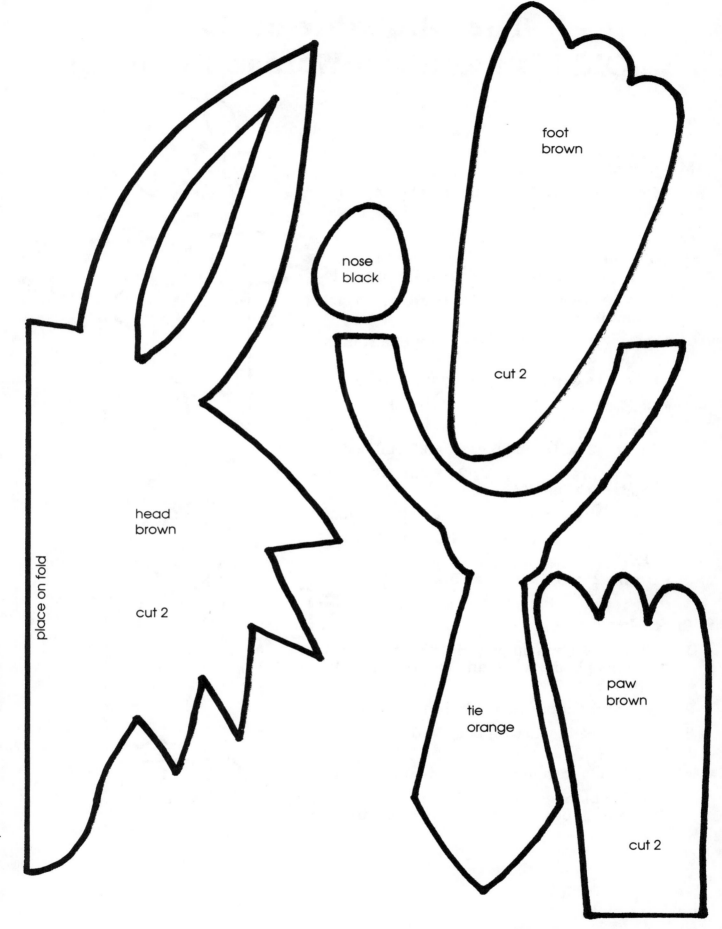

nose
black

foot
brown

cut 2

head
brown

cut 2

place on fold

tie
orange

paw
brown

cut 2

The Gingerbread Boy
(Old Man and Old Woman Puppets)

Figure A

Materials

- One 1" x 10" (2.5 cm x 25.4 cm) cardboard strip for each puppet

Art Paper:

Old Man

- Orange 12" x 18" (30.5 cm x 45.7 cm) body
- Pink or brown 9" x 12" (22.9 cm x 30.5 cm) head, neck, hands
- Gray 6" x 9" (15.2 cm x 22.9 cm) hair, mustache
- Brown 6" x 9" (15.2 cm x 22.9 cm) vest
- Black 2" x 6" (5.0 cm x 15.2 cm) shoes

Old Woman

- Green 12" x 18" (30.5 cm x 45.7 cm) body
- Pink or brown 9" x 12" (22.9 cm x 30.5 cm) head, neck, hands
- Red 6" x 9" (15.2 cm x 22.9 cm) bandana
- White 9" x 12" (22.9 cm x 30.5 cm) hair, apron
- Brown 2" x 6" (5.0 cm x 15.2 cm) shoes

Procedure

1. Follow directions on page 5 for tracing, cutting, and gluing body, head, and cardboard neck strip.*

2. Trace and cut out remaining pattern pieces.

3. Glue pieces in place on body and head (figs. A and B).

4. Add details with markers or crayons.

   *For Old Man, cut an upside-down V shape at the center, bottom of puppet to form pant legs (fig. A).

Figure B

Fables & Tales Papercrafts © 1989 David S. Lake Publishers

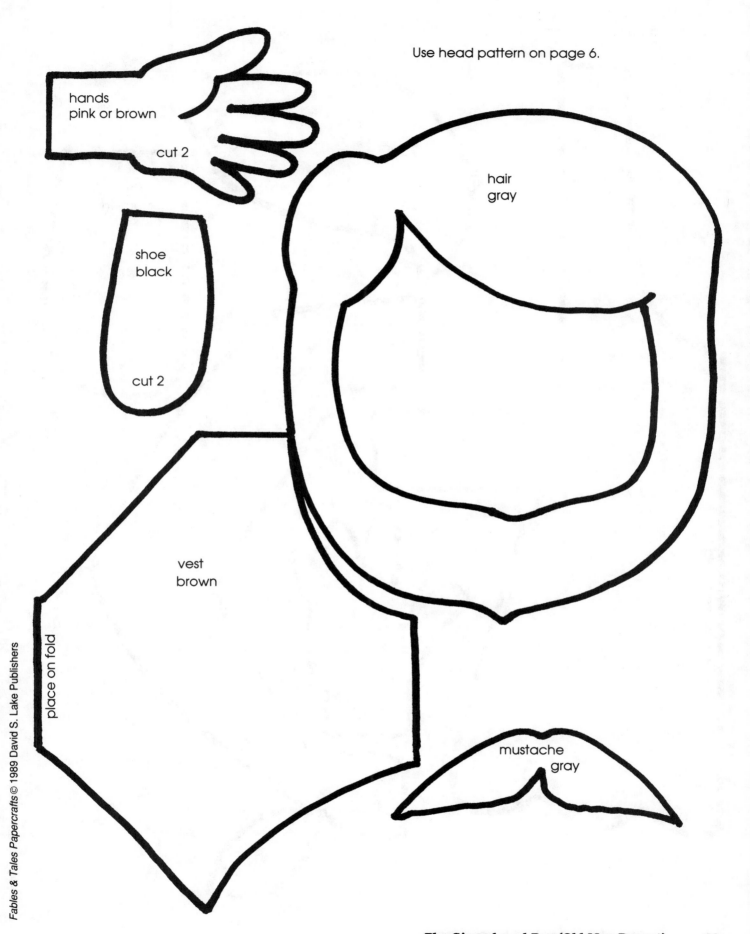

Use head pattern on page 6.

hands
pink or brown

cut 2

hair
gray

shoe
black

cut 2

vest
brown

place on fold

mustache
gray

Fables & Tales Papercrafts © 1989 David S. Lake Publishers

The Gingerbread Boy (Old Man Puppet)   39

Use head pattern on page 6.

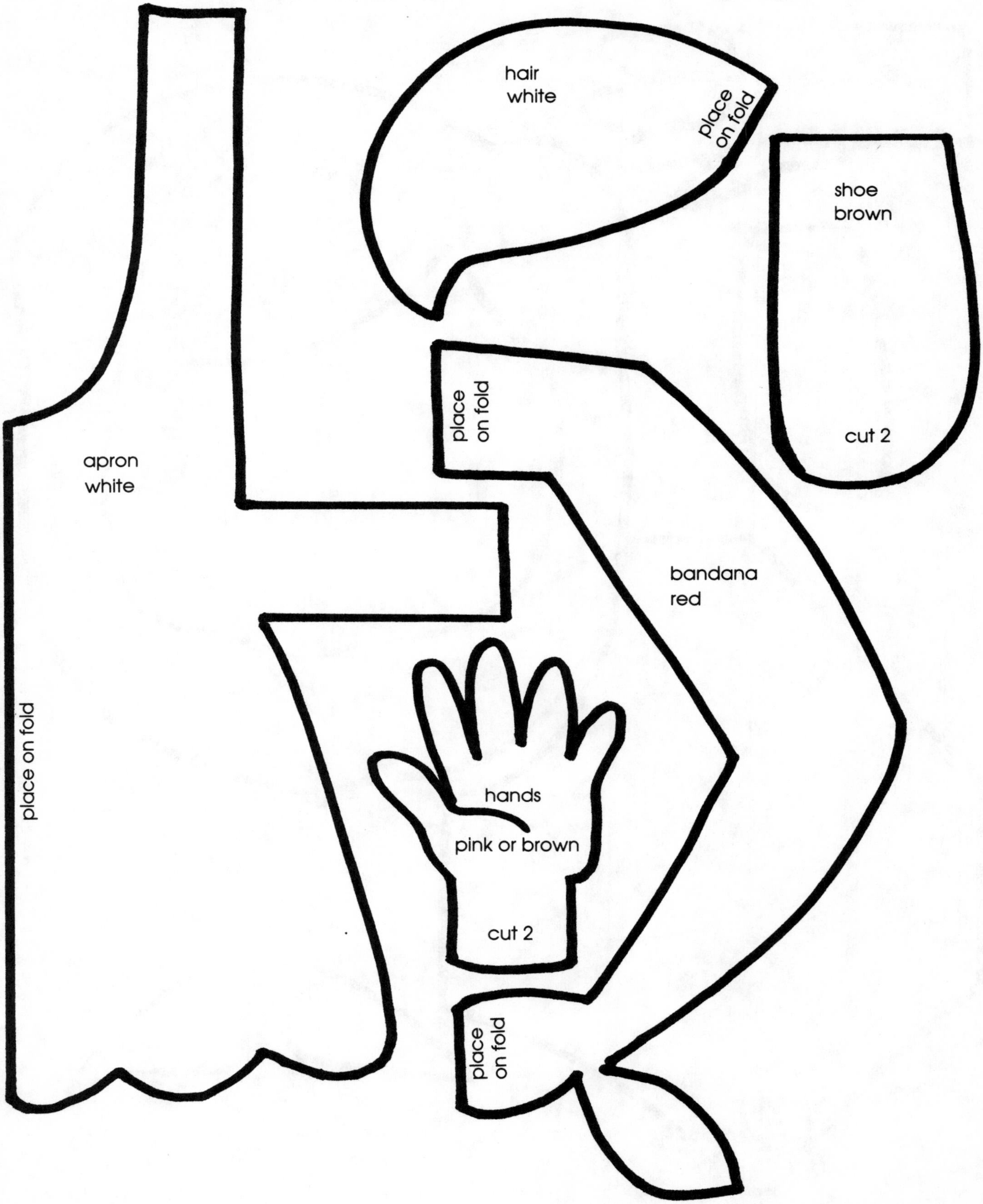

hair
white

place on fold

shoe
brown

cut 2

apron
white

place on fold

place on fold

bandana
red

hands

pink or brown

cut 2

place on fold

Fables & Tales Papercrafts © 1989 David S. Lake Publishers

Little Red Riding Hood

Little Red Riding Hood (Wolf)

Little Red Riding Hood and Wolf Puppets

Figure A

Figure B

Materials

- One 1" x 10" (2.5 cm x 25.4 cm) cardboard strip for each puppet

Art Paper:

Little Red Riding Hood
- Red
    12" x 18" (30.5 cm x 45.7 cm) body
    12" x 18" (30.5 cm x 45.7 cm) cape, hood

- Pink or brown 9" x 12" (22.9 cm x 30.5 cm) head, neck, hands

- Yellow 9" x 12" (22.9 cm x 30.5 cm) basket, hair

- Black 4" x 8" (10.2 cm x 20.3 cm) shoes

- 18" (45.7 cm) white yarn for bows on shoes

Wolf
- Gray
    12" x 18" (30.5 cm x 45.7 cm) body

    12" x 18" (30.5 cm x 45.7 cm) head, neck, paws, feet, tail

- Black scraps for pads on feet and nose

Procedure

1. Follow directions on page 5 for tracing, cutting, and gluing body, head, and cardboard neck strip. (Head for wolf is not cut on the fold.)

2. Trace and cut out remaining pattern pieces.

3. Glue pieces in place on head and body (figs. A and B).

4. Use white yarn to make bows for Little Red Riding Hood's shoes.

5. Add details with black marker or crayon.

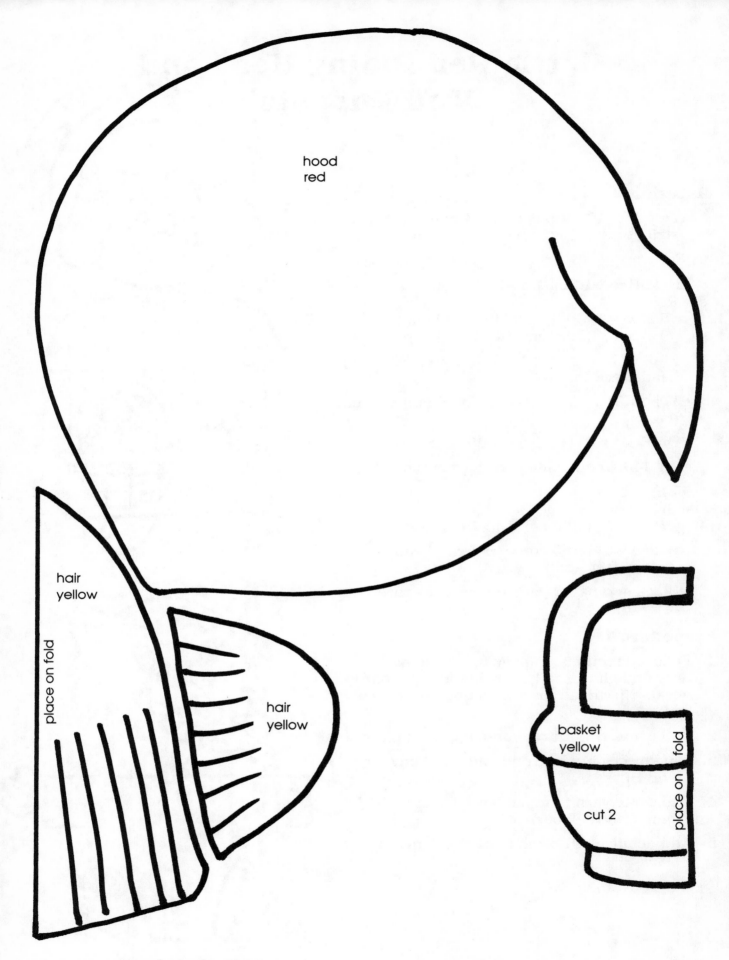

hood
red

hair
yellow

place on fold

hair
yellow

basket
yellow

place on fold

cut 2

Fables & Tales Papercrafts © 1989 David S. Lake Publishers

Little Red Riding Hood Puppet

Use head pattern on page 6.

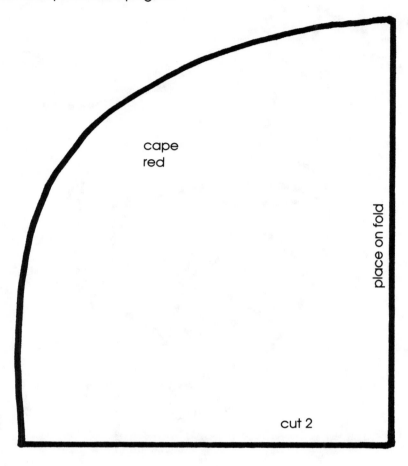

cape
red

place on fold

cut 2

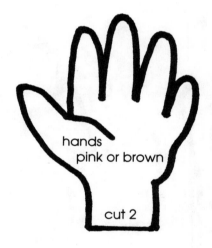

hands
pink or brown

cut 2

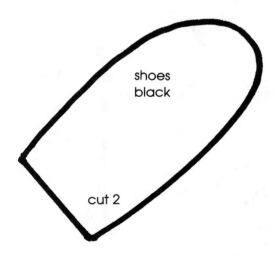

shoes
black

cut 2

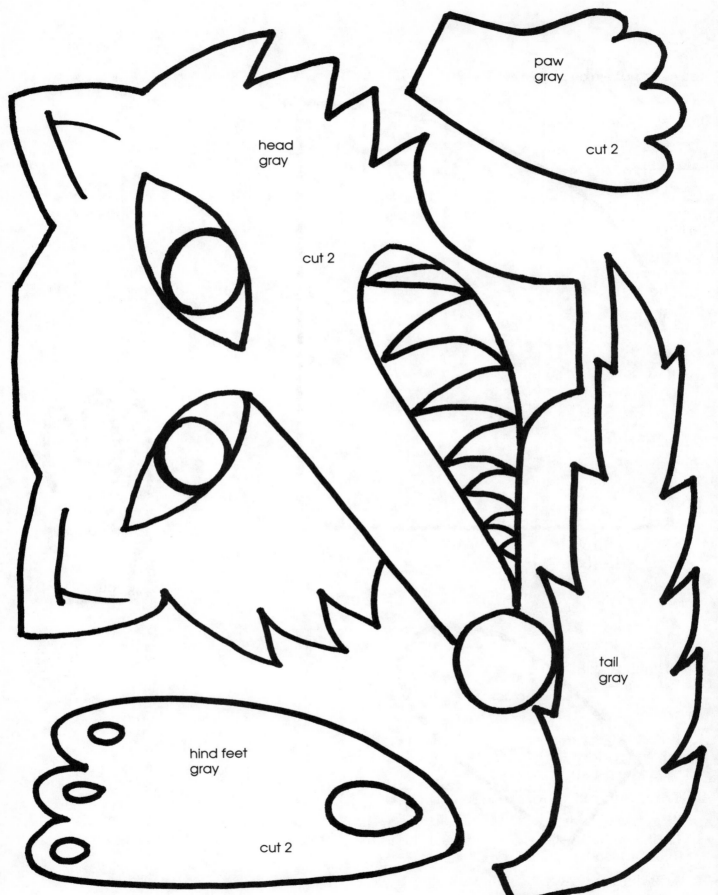

paw
gray

cut 2

head
gray

cut 2

tail
gray

hind feet
gray

cut 2

Little Red Riding Hood (Wolf Puppet)

Little Red Riding Hood
(Mother/Grandmother Puppets)

Figure A

Figure B

Materials

- One 1" x 10" (2.5 cm x 25.4 cm) cardboard strip for each puppet

Art Paper:

Mother

- Green 12" x 18" (30.5 cm x 45.7 cm) body
- Pink or brown
  9" x 12" (22.9 cm x 30.5 cm) head, neck

  3" x 6" (7.6 cm x 15.2 cm) hands
- White 9" x 12" (22.9 cm x 30.5 cm) apron, collar
- Brown 6" x 9" (15.2 cm x 22.9 cm) hair
- Black 2" x 8" (5.0 cm x 20.3 cm) shoes

Grandmother

- Purple 12" x 18" (30.5 cm x 45.7 cm) body
- Pink or brown
  9" x 12" (22.9 cm x 30.5 cm) head, neck

  3" x 6" (7.6 cm x 15.2 cm) hands
- White 12" x 18" (30.5 cm x 45.7 cm) collar, apron, hair
- Black 2" x 8" (5.0 cm x 20.3 cm) shoes

Procedure

1. Follow directions on page 5 for tracing, cutting, and gluing body, head, and cardboard neck strip.
2. Trace and cut out remaining pattern pieces.
3. Glue pieces in place on body and head (figs. A and B).
4. Add details with black marker or crayon.

Fables & Tales Papercrafts © 1989 David S. Lake Publishers

Use head pattern on page 6.

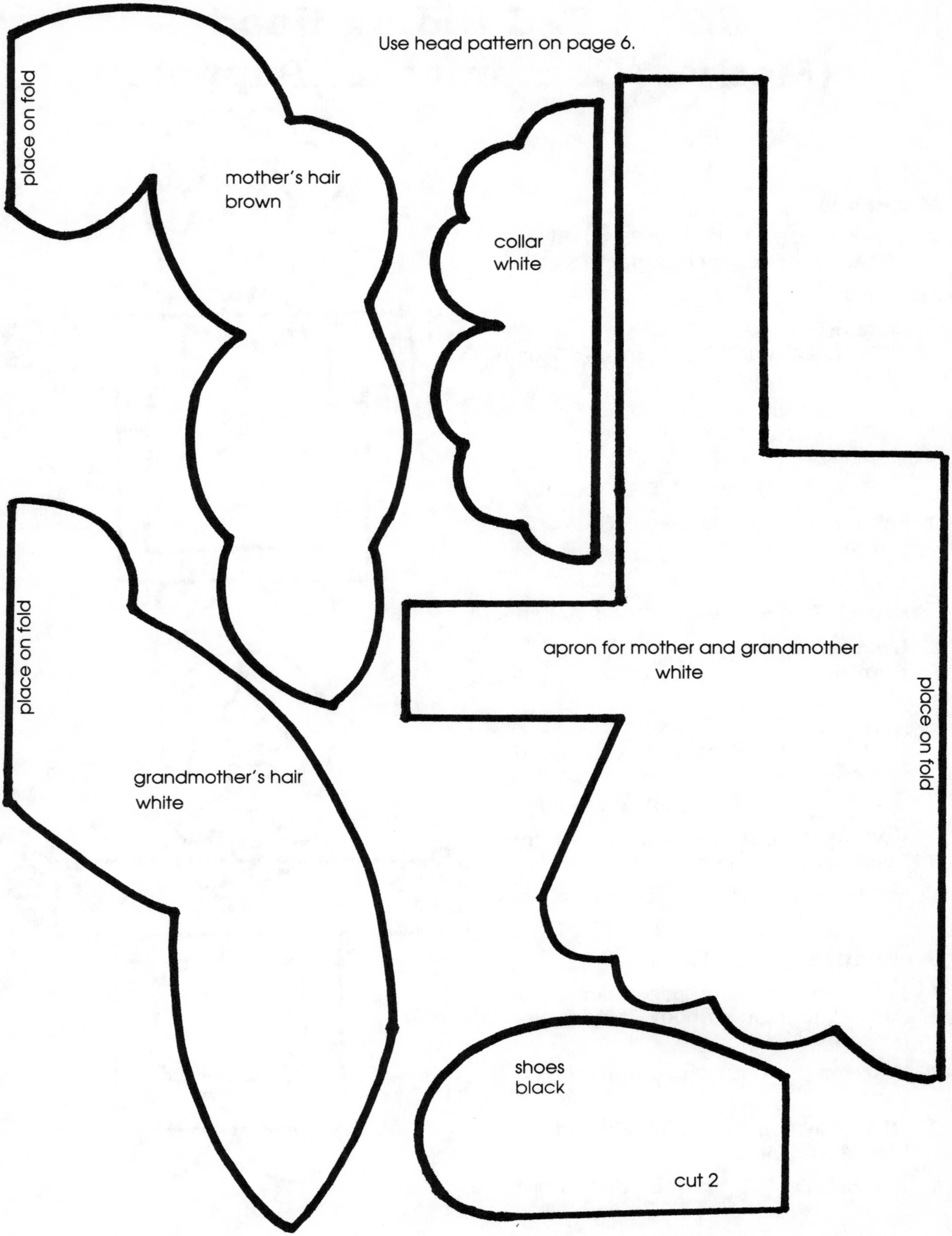

place on fold

mother's hair
brown

collar
white

place on fold

apron for mother and grandmother
white

place on fold

grandmother's hair
white

shoes
black

cut 2

Fables & Tales Papercrafts © 1989 David S. Lake Publishers

Little Red Riding Hood (Mother/Grandmother Puppets)

Little Red Riding Hood
(Woodsman Puppet)

Materials

- One 1" x 10" (2.5 cm x 25.4 cm) card-board strip

Art Paper:

- Orange 12" x 18" (30.5 cm x 45.7 cm) body

- Pink or brown
    9" x 12" (22.9 cm x 30.5 cm) head, neck

    3" x 6" (7.6 cm x 15.2 cm) hands

- Dark blue 4" x 5" (10.2 cm x 12.7 cm) hat

- Black 6" x 9" (15.2 cm x 22.9 cm) shoes, ax

- Light blue 6" x 9" (15.2 cm x 22.9 cm) pants

Figure A

Procedure

1. Follow directions on page 5 for tracing, cutting, and gluing body, head, and card-board neck strip.
2. Trace and cut out remaining pattern pieces.
3. Glue pieces in place (fig. A).
4. Add details with black marker or crayon.

Use head pattern on page 6.

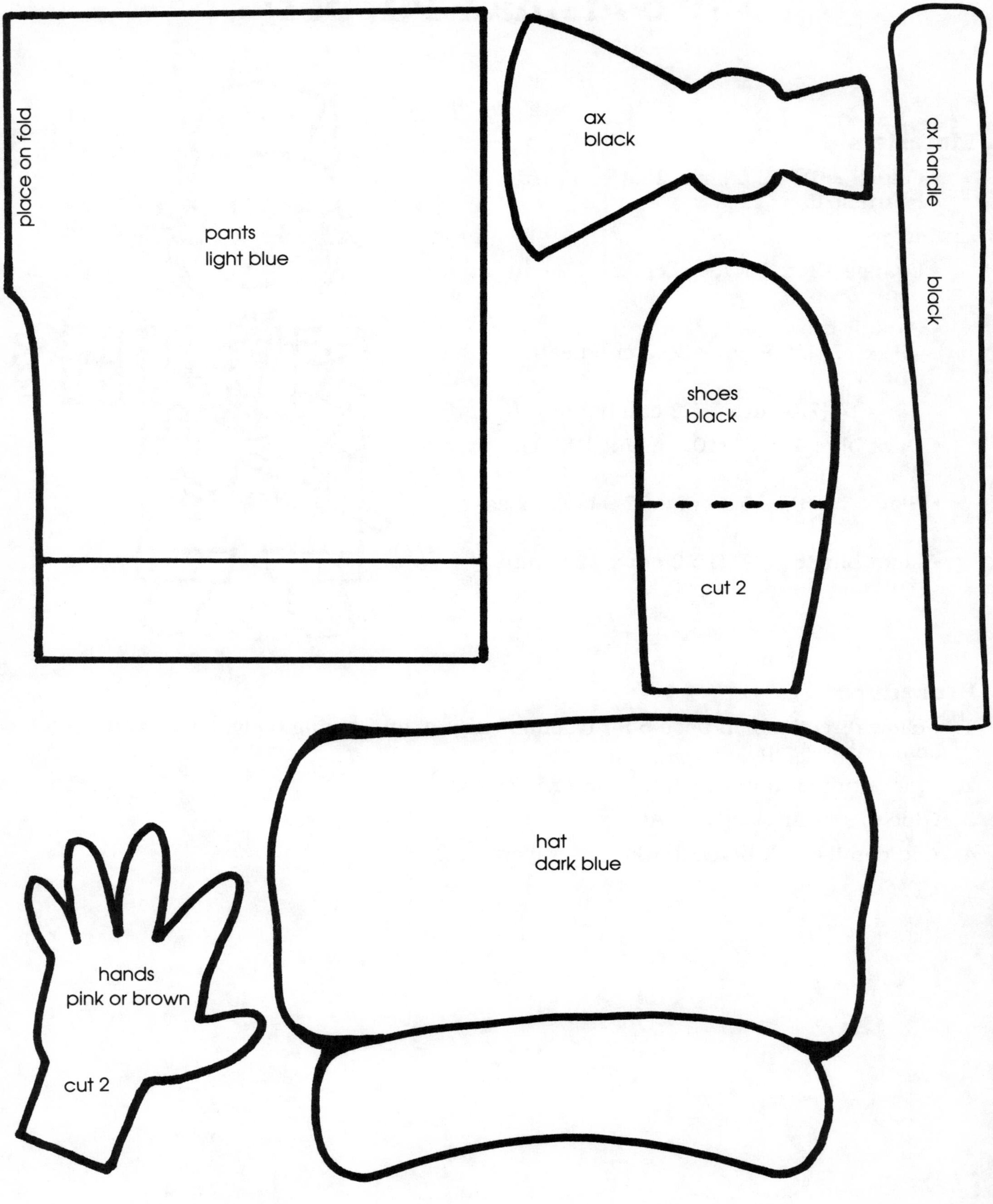

place on fold

pants
light blue

ax
black

ax handle

black

shoes
black

cut 2

hat
dark blue

hands
pink or brown

cut 2

The Three Bears

Goldilocks

Fables & Tales Papercrafts © 1989 David S. Lake Publishers

The Three Bears
(Goldilocks and Mama Bear Puppets)

Figure A

Figure B

Materials

- One 1" x 10" (2.5 cm x 25.4 cm) cardboard strip for each puppet

Art Paper:

Goldilocks

- Green 12" x 18" (30.5 cm x 45.7 cm) body
- Pink or brown 12" x 18" (30.5 cm x 45.7 cm) head, neck, hands
- Black 6" x 9" (15.2 cm x 22.9 cm) bow, shoes
- Four 1" x 6" (2.5 cm x 15.2 cm) yellow strips for hair

Mama Bear

- Brown
  12" x 18" (30.5 cm x 45.7 cm) body
  12" x 18" (30.5 cm x 45.7 cm) head, neck
  6" x 9" (15.2 cm x 22.9 cm) paws, feet
- White 9" x 12" (22.9 cm x 30.5 cm) apron
- Black, white, pink scraps for inner ears, eyes, nose, muzzle

Procedure

1. Follow directions on page 5 for tracing, cutting, and gluing body, head, and cardboard neck strip.
2. Trace and cut out remaining pattern pieces.
3. Glue pieces in place on body and head (figs. A and B).*
4. Add details with markers, crayons, or scraps.

   *Curl yellow strips between pencil and thumb for locks of Goldilock's hair.

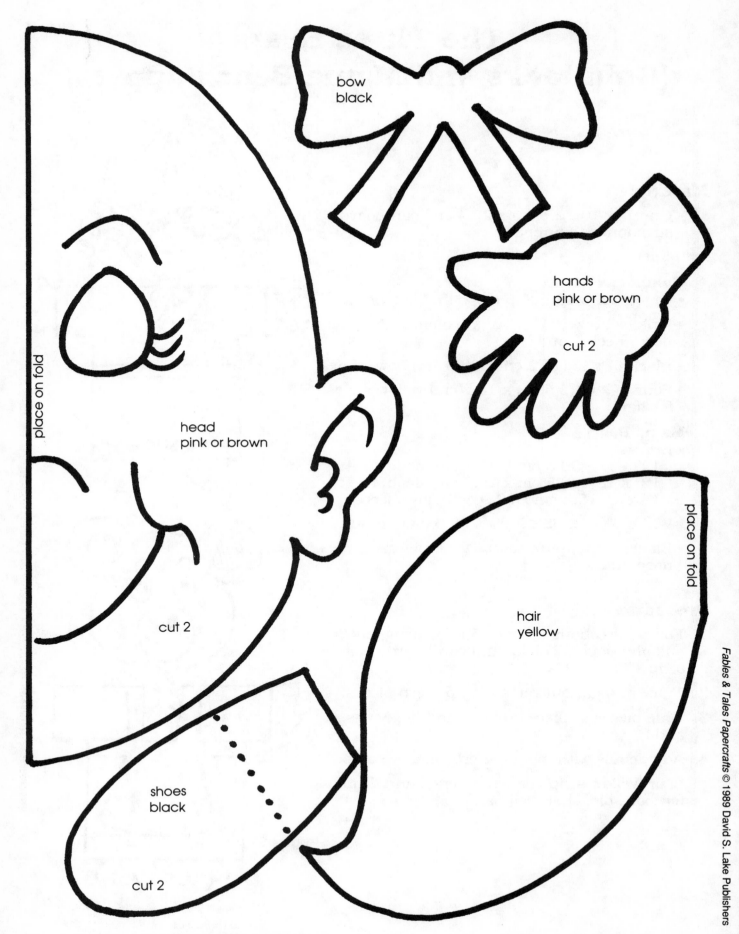

place on fold

bow
black

hands
pink or brown

cut 2

head
pink or brown

cut 2

place on fold

hair
yellow

shoes
black

cut 2

Fables & Tales Papercrafts © 1989 David S. Lake Publishers

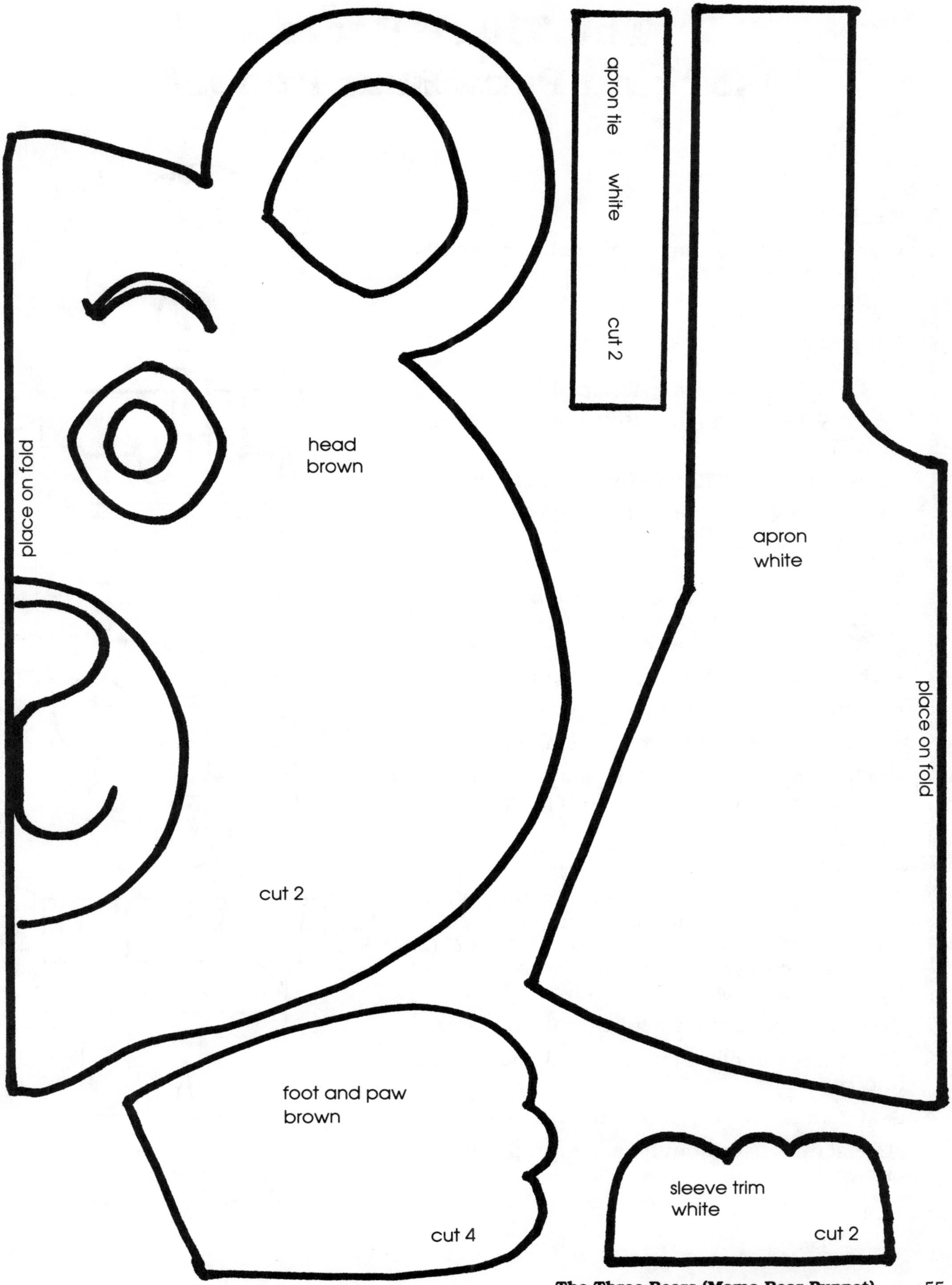

apron tie   white   cut 2

head
brown

place on fold

apron
white

place on fold

cut 2

foot and paw
brown

sleeve trim
white

cut 4

cut 2

The Three Bears
(Baby and Papa Bear Puppets)

Figure A

Figure B

Materials

- One .1" x 10" (2.5 cm x 25.4 cm) cardboard strip for each puppet

Art Paper:

Baby Bear
- Brown
    12" x 18" (30.5 cm x 45.7 cm) body

    12" x 18" (30.5 cm x 45.7 cm) head, neck, paws, feet

- Green 9" x 12" (22.9 cm x 30.5 cm) coveralls

- Pink 3" x 4" (7.6 cm x 10.2 cm) muzzle

Papa Bear
- Brown
    12" x 18" (30.5 cm x 45.7 cm) body
    12" x 18" (30.5 cm x 45.7 cm) head, neck
    6" x 9" (15.2 cm x 22.9 cm) paws, feet

- Blue 9" x 12" (22.9 cm x 30.5 cm) coveralls

- White 5" x 8" (12.7 cm x 20.3 cm) shirt

- Pink 4" x 5" (10.2 cm x 12.7 cm) muzzle

- Yellow, black, white, pink scraps for eyes, buttons, nose, inner ears for both puppets*

Procedure

1. Follow directions on page 5 for tracing, cutting, and gluing body, head, and cardboard neck strip. (For baby bear, trim folded 9 " x 12" (22.9 cm x 30.5 cm) to 8" x 11" (20.3 cm x 27.9 cm) before continuing to make body.)

2. Trace and cut out remaining pattern pieces.

3. Glue pieces in place on head and body (figs. A and B).

4. Add details with black marker or crayon.

   *Use scraps to cut out small, appropriate size circles or ovals.

Fables & Tales Papercrafts © 1989 David S. Lake Publishers

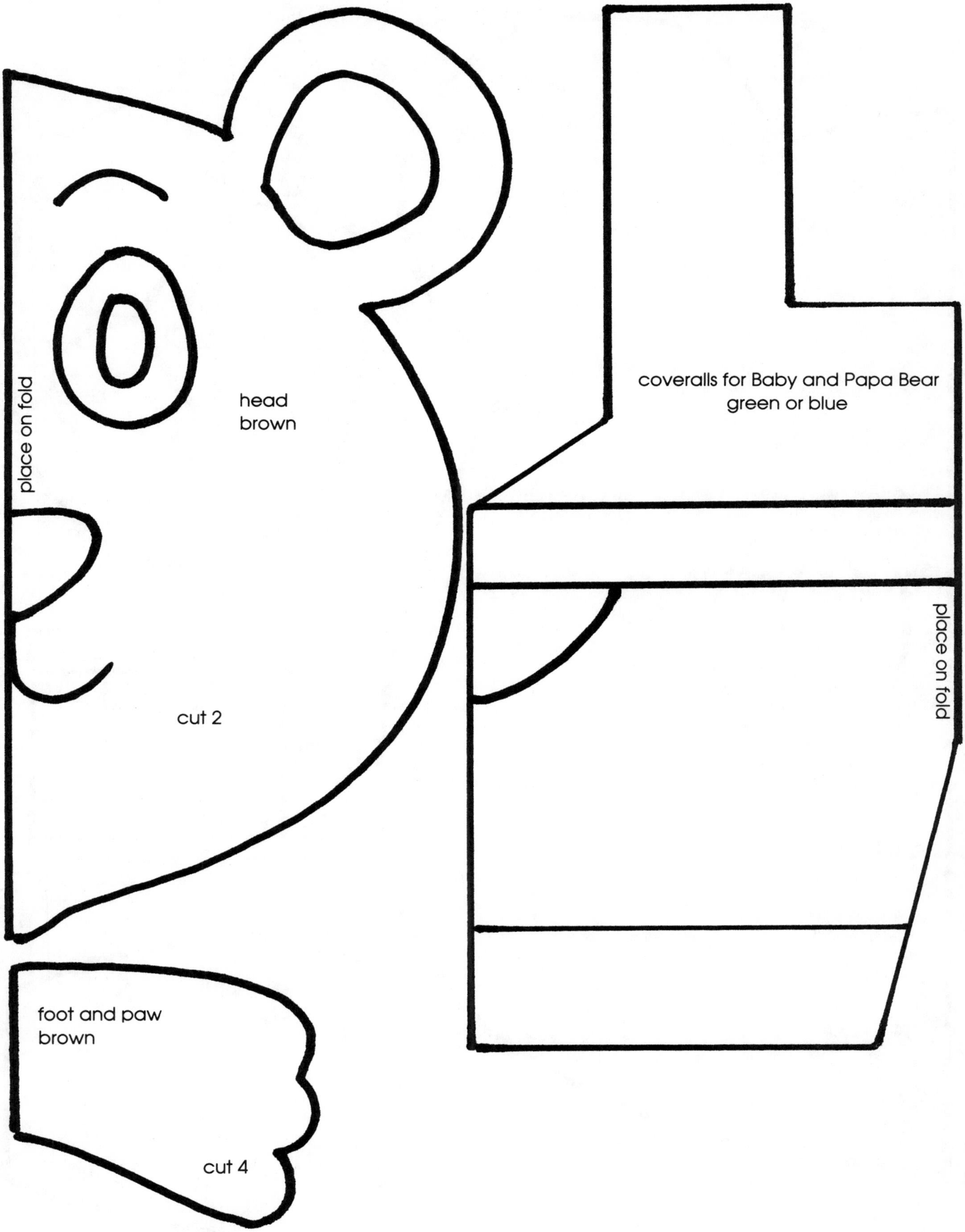

place on fold

head
brown

cut 2

coveralls for Baby and Papa Bear
green or blue

place on fold

foot and paw
brown

cut 4

The Three Bears (Baby Bear Puppet)   57

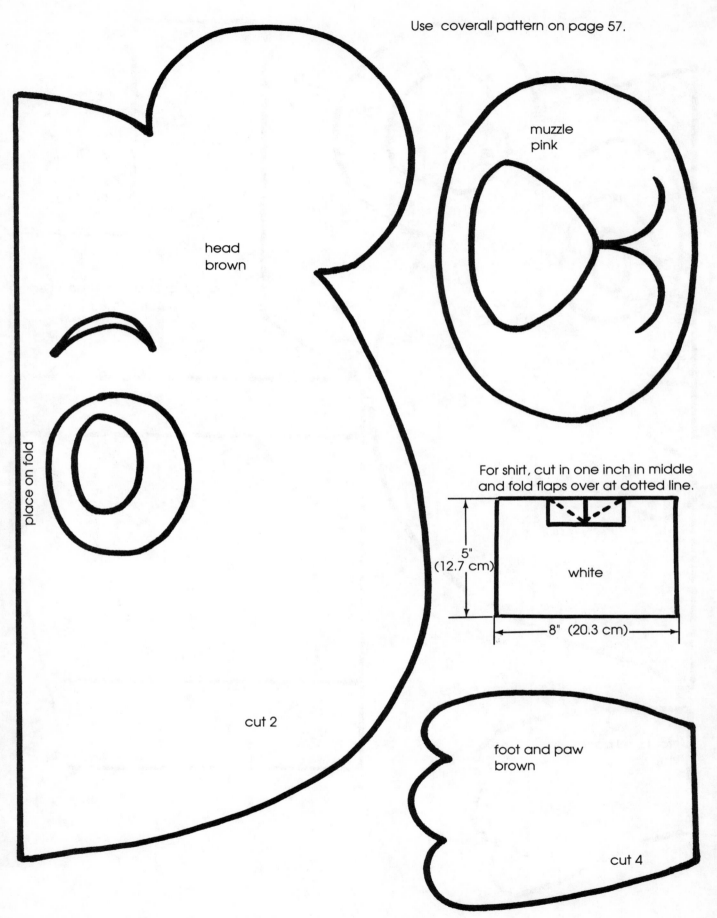

Use coverall pattern on page 57.

muzzle
pink

head
brown

place on fold

cut 2

For shirt, cut in one inch in middle
and fold flaps over at dotted line.

5"
(12.7 cm)

white

8" (20.3 cm)

foot and paw
brown

cut 4

Fables & Tales Papercrafts © 1989 David S. Lake Publishers

The Three Little Pigs

The Three Little Pigs (Wolf)

The Three Little Pigs
(Pigs and Wolf Masks)

Materials

- One 1" x 10" (2.5 cm x 25.4 cm) cardboard strip for each mask

Art Paper:

For each pig

- Pink 12" x 18" (30.5 cm x 45.7 cm) head, neck
- White 4" x 4" (10.2 cm x 10.2 cm) muzzle
- Add for pig #2—Blue 3" x 4" (7.6 cm x 10.2 cm) cap
- Add for pig #3—Yellow 9" x 12" (22.9 cm x 30.5 cm) hat

Wolf

- Brown
  12" x 18" (30.5 cm x 45.7 cm) head, neck
  6" x 9" (15.2 cm x 22.9 cm) ears
- Pink 6" x 9" (15.2 cm x 22.9 cm) inner ears, tongue

Procedure

1. Follow directions on page 7 for tracing, cutting, and gluing head and cardboard neck strip.
2. Trace and cut out remaining pattern pieces.
3. Glue pieces in place on head (figs. A, B, C, and D).
4. Add details with markers or crayons.

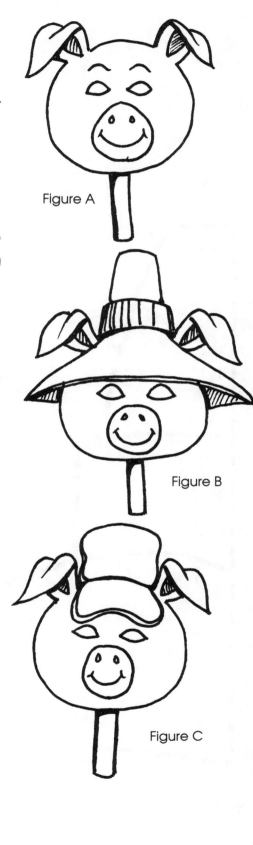

Figure A

Figure B

Figure C

Figure D

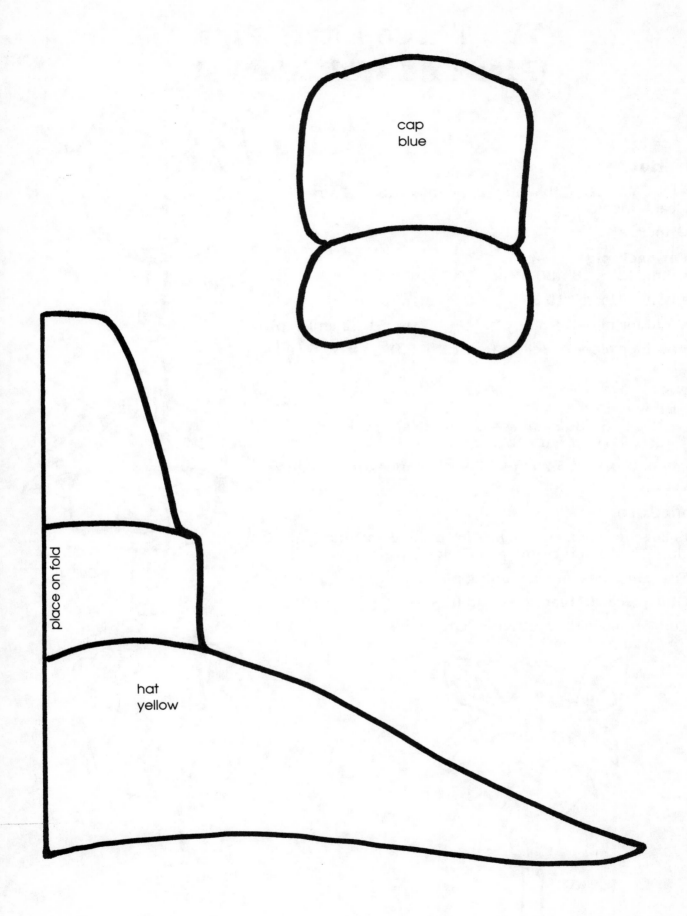

cap
blue

place on fold

hat
yellow

head
pink

place on fold

cut 2

muzzle
pink

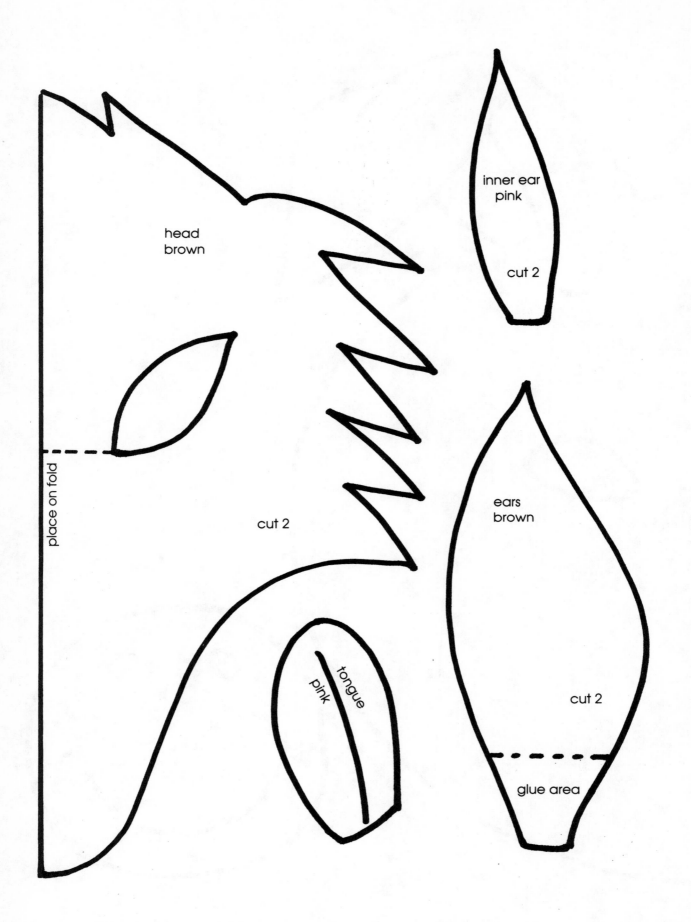

inner ear
pink

cut 2

head
brown

ears
brown

place on fold

cut 2

cut 2

tongue
pink

glue area

Fables & Tales Papercrafts © 1989 David S. Lake Publishers